Plant Top Tens

North America's Most Amazing Plants

www.raintreepublishers.co.uk
Visit our website to find out more information about Raintree Books.

To order:
☎ Phone 44 (o) 1865 888112
▤ Send a fax to 44 (o) 1865 314091
▭ Visit the Raintree Bookshop at **www.raintreepublishers.co.uk** to browse our catalogue and order online

Raintree is an imprint of Capstone Global Library Limited, a company incorporated in England and Wales having its registered office at 7 Pilgrim Street, London, EC4V 6LB – Registered company number: 6695582

"Raintree" is a registered trademark of Pearson Education Limited, under licence to Capstone Global Library Limited

Text © Capstone Global Library Limited 2008
First published in hardback in 2008
First published in paperback in 2009

Produced for Raintree by Calcium

Editorial: Kate de Villiers and Sarah Eason
Design: Victoria Bevan and Paul Myerscough
Illustrations: Geoff Ward
Picture Research: Maria Joannou
Originated by Modern Age
Printed and bound by China Translation Printing Services

ISBN 978 1 4062 0971 6 (hardback)
12 11 10 09 08
10 9 8 7 6 5 4 3 2 1

ISBN 978 1 4062 0978 5 (paperback)
13 12 11 10 09
10 9 8 7 6 5 4 3 2 1

British Library Cataloguing in Publication Data
Scott, Michael and Royston, Angela
    North America. - (Plant top tens)
    581.9'7
A full catalogue record for this book is available from the British Library.

Acknowledgements
The authors and publisher are grateful to the following for permission to reproduce copyright material: © Ardea p. 17 (John Cancalosi); © FLPA pp. 14 (Carr Clifton/ Minden Pictures), 19 (Mark Newman), 20 (Fritz Polking); © iStockphoto pp. 4, 8, 11, 13, 23; © Library of Congress p. 7; © Nature Picture Library p. 15 (Barry Mansell); © NHPA p. 18 (John Shaw); © Photolibrary pp. 6 (Breck P. Kent), 10 (Lynn Keddie), 12 (Garden Picture Library/ John Glover), 24 (Oxford Scientific Films/Richard Herrmann), 25 (Animals Animals), 27 (Alaskastock/ Michael DeYoung); © Science Photo Library p. 21 (Robert J. Erwin); © Shutterstock pp. 9 (Jennifer Leigh Selig), 16 (Nelson Sirlin), 22; © Dieter Wilken p. 26.

Cover photograph of a bristlecone pine reproduced with permission of Getty Images/Lonely Planet.

Every effort has been made to contact copyright holders of any material reproduced in this book. Any omissions will be rectified in subsequent printings if notice is given to the publishers.

Contents

Some words are printed in bold, **like this**. You can find out what they mean on page 31 in the Glossary.

North America

North America stretches from the **Arctic Ocean** in the north to the **deserts** of Mexico. The land around the Arctic Ocean is frozen for most of the year. The deserts are hot and dry. The **continent** also has huge forests of pine trees, **swamps**, mountains, and other **habitats**.

The high Rocky Mountains stretch from one end of North America to the other.

Species

A **species** is a type of living thing. About 5,000 species of plant grow in Canada, and about 20,000 species of plant grow in the United States. The islands of Hawaii in the Pacific Ocean have another 1,000 species of plant.

Key
- evergreen forest
- desert
- grassland
- mountains
- tundra
- borderlines

N
W   E
S

0   1,000 miles
0   1,000 kilometres

Alaska

CANADA

Great Lakes

Pacific Ocean

Missouri River

UNITED STATES

Appalachian
Mountains

Mississippi River

Atlantic Ocean

The Everglades

North America

Mexico

Much of North America is covered by grassland or forest.

Each habitat is home to different types of plant and animal. Some plants grow best in a particular habitat. They have features that make them suited to their habitat. Some of the most amazing plants are found in the most difficult habitats.

Giant sequoia

The giant sequoia is the most massive tree in the world. It is not the tallest tree, but it is the heaviest. It weighs more than 1,000 elephants! Its trunk is so thick it would take nearly 20 people holding hands to reach around it. The trees grow so big because they live for thousands of years.

This giant sequoia is the heaviest tree in the world. It is called "General Sherman".

Protected by bark

Giant sequoias grow in just a few places in the hills near the Sierra Nevada mountains. These hillsides are often struck by lightning and catch fire, but the giant sequoias do not burn. Their thick **bark** protects them from the flames.

GIANT SEQUOIA

HEIGHT:
OVER 90 METRES (300 FEET)

LIFESPAN:
UP TO 3,500 YEARS

HABITAT:
MOUNTAIN WOODLAND

THAT'S AMAZING!
IF "GENERAL SHERMAN" WAS CUT UP INTO WOODEN PLANKS AND THOSE PLANKS WERE LAID END TO END, THEY WOULD STRETCH FOR 1,800 KILOMETRES (1,100 MILES).

North America

Pacific Ocean

Atlantic Ocean

where giant sequoias are found

A tunnel was cut through the trunk of this giant sequoia. The tree fell down 88 years later.

Bristlecone pine

The oldest tree in the world is a bristlecone pine. It is about 4,770 years old. It began to grow when the Ancient Egyptians were building their pyramids.

Growing slowly

Bristlecone pines live so long because they grow very slowly. Even when part of the tree dies, the tree's strong **roots** stop it falling over. The rest of the tree keeps on growing.

Tree rings

Each year a layer of new wood grows below the bark. When the tree is cut down the layers show as rings. Counting the rings gives the age of the tree.

Bristlecone pines are not very tall but they can live for thousands of years.

BRISTLECONE PINE

HEIGHT:
UP TO 18 METRES (60 FEET)

LIFESPAN:
AT LEAST 4,000 YEARS

HABITAT:
HIGH MOUNTAIN FORESTS

THAT'S AMAZING!
SCIENTISTS FOUND OUT THE AGE OF THE OLDEST TREE BY DRILLING OUT A NARROW TUBE OF WOOD AND COUNTING ITS RINGS.

North America

Pacific Ocean

Atlantic Ocean

where bristlecone pines are found

Part of this bristlecone pine is dead, but its roots hold it steady in the ground.

Mountain tree

Bristlecone pines grow high up in the mountains. Here there is only a little rain each year, and it is almost always windy. The winter is freezing cold and the summer is very short. The tree grows just a little bit each year.

Venus flytrap

A venus flytrap traps and eats insects! It has a circle of leaves around the bottom of its **stem**. These leaves are divided in two, with a hinge between them. The edges of the leaves are lined with sharp spines. When a fly lands on the leaf, the hinge closes the leaf. The spines trap the fly like the bars of a cage!

The leaves of a venus flytrap make a sugary juice. This juice attracts the flies.

Eating flies

Venus flytraps grow in damp places where the soil is poor. The plant gets extra **nutrients** from the flies. When a fly is trapped, the leaf makes a strong liquid. This liquid slowly breaks down the fly into tiny pieces. It takes about ten days for the plant to break down and eat the fly. Then the leaf opens again.

The leaf snaps shut, trapping the fly.

VENUS FLYTRAP

HEIGHT:
UP TO 30 CENTIMETRES
(12 INCHES) TALL

LIFESPAN:
SEVERAL YEARS

HABITAT:
BOGS AND DAMP MOSSY PLACES

THAT'S AMAZING!
A VENUS FLYTRAP SNAPS SHUT
IN LESS THAN HALF A SECOND.

North America

Pacific Ocean

Atlantic Ocean

where venus flytraps are found

Sugar maple

In autumn, the leaves of sugar maples turn bright red. Then they change to orange and yellow before they fall. Many trees have leaves that change colour, but the sugar maple is the most colourful. That is because the leaves contain a dye that turns them red. This dye may help to keep the leaves alive, while the tree sucks their fluid back into its trunk.

In autumn the leaves of sugar maple trees change colour and fall to the ground.

Falling leaves

Most trees with broad, flat leaves drop their leaves in autumn. They do this to protect themselves from the cold winter weather. Their thin leaves could easily be damaged by frost.

Sugary juice

Sugar maples make a thick, sweet juice, called maple syrup. In the past, a hole was drilled in the trunk and the syrup was collected in buckets. Today, plastic pipes carry the syrup straight to factories.

SUGAR MAPLE

HEIGHT:
UP TO 40 METRES
(130 FEET)

LIFESPAN:
200 YEARS OR MORE

HABITAT:
FORESTS

THAT'S AMAZING!
IT TAKES 25–32 LITRES OF JUICE FROM A SUGAR MAPLE TREE TO MAKE 1 LITRE OF MAPLE SYRUP.

North America

Pacific Ocean

Atlantic Ocean

where sugar maples are found

Maple syrup is being collected from this sugar maple tree.

Century plant

Century plants grow well in deserts. Their huge leaves store water when it finally rains. The leathery surface of the leaves keeps in the water. The leaves store sugary food as well as water. This sugar gives the plant energy. The edges of the leaves are covered with sharp spines to stop animals eating them.

The leaves of a century plant form a circle on the ground.

Super stem

After 10 to 25 years, a century plant suddenly grows a tall flower stem. This stem has many branches with hundreds of tiny flowers. Hummingbirds, moths, and bats visit the flowers and take the **pollen** from one flower to another. Growing the flowers takes all of the plant's energy. When the flowers have made their **seeds**, the plant dies.

CENTURY PLANT

HEIGHT:
FLOWER UP TO 12 METRES
(40 FEET) TALL

LIFESPAN:
10–25 YEARS

HABITAT:
DESERT

THAT'S AMAZING!
THE CENTURY PLANT GETS ITS NAME BECAUSE PEOPLE USED TO THINK IT LIVED FOR A CENTURY (100 YEARS) BEFORE IT FLOWERED.

where century plants are found

North America

Atlantic Ocean

Pacific Ocean

Pollen sticks to this bat as it moves from flower to flower.

Saguaro cactus

The saguaro cactus is one of the world's biggest cacti, but it grows very slowly. During the first 10 years of its life, it may grow only 4 centimetres (less than 2 inches)! It can take 30 years to reach 1 metre (3 feet) and 50 years to produce its first flowers.

Saguaro cacti grow only in the Sonoran Desert.

SAGUARO CACTUS

HEIGHT:
UP TO 15 METRES
(50 FEET) TALL

LIFESPAN:
200 YEARS OR MORE

HABITAT:
SONORAN DESERT

THAT'S AMAZING!
DURING A RAINSTORM, A SAGUARO CACTUS CAN TAKE IN AND STORE MORE THAN A TONNE OF WATER. THAT'S ENOUGH TO FILL FOUR BATHS.

North America

Pacific Ocean

Atlantic Ocean

where saguaro cacti are found

This owl is nesting in a hole in the stem of a saguaro cactus. The hole was made by a woodpecker, whose long beak can reach between the sharp spines.

Water stores

Saguaro cacti grow in the Sonoran Desert in the south-west of the United States and north-west of Mexico. This desert gets some rain, but it is very hot. The saguaro takes in water when it rains and stores it in its huge stem. The stem swells when it is filled with water, and slowly shrinks during the dry seasons. The stem is covered with sharp spines. They stop animals from drinking its store of water.

Arctic lupin

The beautiful Arctic lupin grows in the wild in the far north of North America. Here the winters are long and dark. The ground is covered with snow for most of the year. When the snow melts, the ground becomes a wet **meadow**. The summer lasts only a few weeks. Then Arctic lupins grow and the flowers quickly make seeds.

Arctic year

In the Arctic it hardly gets light at all in winter. In summer it never gets dark. However, the summer Sun is so weak it takes a long time to melt the snow. Sometimes it does not melt at all.

Arctic lupins grow in one of the harshest habitats in North America.

Bursting pods

When the seeds are ripe, the **pod** bursts open. The seeds fly in all directions. Sometimes the seeds lie under the snow for many years before the snow melts. Then they begin to grow.

ARCTIC LUPIN

HEIGHT:
UP TO 50 CENTIMETRES
(20 INCHES)

LIFESPAN:
A FEW YEARS

HABITAT:
ARCTIC MEADOWS
AND HILLSIDES

THAT'S AMAZING!
THE SEEDS OF ARCTIC LUPINS LAST LONGER THAN THOSE OF OTHER PLANTS. SOME SEEDS WERE FOUND THAT WERE 10,000 YEARS OLD. WHEN THEY WERE PLANTED, THEY GREW.

Most of the flowers of the Arctic lupin are purplish-blue, but a few of them are pink.

North America

Pacific Ocean

Atlantic Ocean

where Arctic lupins are found

Poison ivy

Poison ivy looks harmless but it can be very dangerous. Every part of the plant contains **poisonous** oil. If a person touches the plant, the poison can make their skin red and itchy. It can also make their skin blister. However, some animals are unharmed by its poison. For example, deer eat poison ivy and birds spread their seeds.

The leaves of the poison ivy have three flaps.

Not an ivy

Poison ivy looks like ivy, but in fact it is not. Like ivy, it often climbs up other plants. It is covered in small, yellowish-white flowers between May and July. It looks most attractive in autumn, when its leaves turn red. Poison ivy grows in woods and other places. It can be hard to see because it creeps around other plants.

Poison ivy flowers produce white berries.

POISON IVY

HEIGHT:
UP TO 1.5 METRES (5 FEET), BUT CAN GROW HIGHER UP ANOTHER PLANT

LIFESPAN:
SEVERAL YEARS

HABITAT:
WOODS, WASTE GROUND, ROADSIDES, AND HEDGEROWS

THAT'S AMAZING!
BURNING POISON IVY DOES NOT DESTROY ITS POISON. THE SMOKE FROM THE DRIED STEMS MAKES PEOPLE'S EYES SWELL SHUT.

North America

Pacific Ocean

Atlantic Ocean

□ where poison ivies are found

Highbush blueberry

Highbush blueberry grows in swamps and boggy woods. Here the soil is very **acid**. Most plants do not like acid soil, but blueberries grow well in it. Highbush blueberry is the wild plant from which other blueberries were specially grown, or **cultivated**.

North America

Pacific Ocean

Atlantic Ocean

where highbush blueberries are found

Wild blueberries taste sweet and tangy.

Cultivating plants

Farmers cultivate plants. They choose the seeds from plants that produce the biggest berries. These seeds then grow into new plants with big, juicy berries.

These berries will be made into jam, muffins, and other foods.

Juicy berries

Blueberries have small flowers shaped like bells. They produce juicy berries between June and August. Animals and people love to eat blueberries. In autumn, birds, foxes, skunks, and other animals feed on the berries. In winter, rabbits and deer eat the leaves and twigs.

Giant kelp

Giant kelp is the world's largest seaweed. Its long leaves are called **fronds**. Many fronds grow close together, forming a huge forest. The tips of the fronds spread out over the surface of the sea. These tips contain small balloons of air that keep them afloat.

Giant kelp grows in clear water near the coast.

GIANT KELP

SIZE:
UP TO 50 METRES
(164 FEET) LONG

LIFESPAN:
SEVERAL YEARS

HABITAT:
CLEAR SEA WATER

THAT'S AMAZING!
GIANT KELP
GROWS VERY
FAST. A FROND
CAN GROW
60 CENTIMETRES
(24 INCHES) IN
A DAY.

North
America

Pacific
Ocean

Atlantic
Ocean

where giant
kelp is found

Holding On

A giant kelp grows from a **holdfast**. This is a tangle of tough strands that grow around a rock. The holdfast holds the fronds of kelp tightly to the rock, so that storms do not wash them away. Fish and many sea animals live in a kelp forest. Crabs, worms, and starfish live in the holdfasts.

Seaweeds

Seaweeds are not true plants. Like plants, they need sunlight to survive and grow. Unlike plants, they do not have roots.

This sea otter is having a nap. It has wrapped itself in giant kelp so that the waves do not wash it away!

Plants in danger

Many plants in North America are in danger of becoming **extinct**. This means that soon none of them will grow in the wild. Plants become extinct for different reasons. For example, only 50 ventura marsh milk-vetch plants were still growing wild in 1997. They all grew on one piece of waste land. Scientists are now trying to get the plant to grow on another site, to stop it becoming extinct.

Ventura marsh milk-vetch plants grew only on a disused oilfield in California.

In the wild, sitka spruces grow up to 90 metres (300 feet) tall.

Sitka spruces grow wild only on the west coast of North America. The wood of sitka spruces is very valuable. It is so valuable that most of the wild trees have been cut down. Wild sitka spruces are now quite rare in North America, but they are planted in many places in northern Europe. They are planted in big forests called **plantations**. They are cut down when they are only 30 metres (100 feet) tall and their wood is sold.

Plant facts and figures

There are millions of different kinds of plants growing all over the world. The place where a plant lives is called its habitat. Plants have special features, such as flowers, leaves, and stems. These features allow plants to survive in their habitats. Which plant do you think is the most amazing?

GIANT SEQUOIA

HEIGHT:
OVER 90 METRES
(300 FEET)

LIFESPAN:
UP TO 3,500 YEARS

HABITAT:
MOUNTAIN WOODLAND

THAT'S AMAZING!
IF "GENERAL SHERMAN" WAS CUT UP INTO WOODEN PLANKS AND THOSE PLANKS WERE LAID END TO END, THEY WOULD STRETCH FOR 1,800 KILOMETRES (1,100 MILES).

BRISTLECONE PINE

HEIGHT:
UP TO 18 METRES (60 FEET)

LIFESPAN:
AT LEAST 4,000 YEARS

HABITAT:
HIGH MOUNTAIN FORESTS

THAT'S AMAZING!
SCIENTISTS FOUND OUT THE AGE OF THE OLDEST TREE BY DRILLING OUT A NARROW TUBE OF WOOD AND COUNTING ITS RINGS.

VENUS FLYTRAP

HEIGHT:
UP TO 30 CENTIMETRES (12 INCHES) TALL

LIFESPAN:
SEVERAL YEARS

HABITAT:
BOGS AND DAMP MOSSY PLACES

THAT'S AMAZING!
A VENUS FLYTRAP SNAPS SHUT IN LESS THAN HALF A SECOND.

SUGAR MAPLE

HEIGHT:
UP TO 40 METRES (130 FEET)

LIFESPAN:
200 YEARS OR MORE

HABITAT:
FORESTS

THAT'S AMAZING!
IT TAKES 25–32 LITRES OF JUICE FROM A SUGAR MAPLE TREE TO MAKE 1 LITRE OF MAPLE SYRUP.

CENTURY PLANT

HEIGHT:
FLOWER UP TO 12 METRES (40 FEET) TALL

LIFESPAN:
10–25 YEARS

HABITAT:
DESERT

THAT'S AMAZING!
THE CENTURY PLANT GETS ITS NAME BECAUSE PEOPLE USED TO THINK IT LIVED FOR A CENTURY (100 YEARS) BEFORE IT FLOWERED.

SAGUARO CACTUS

HEIGHT:
UP TO 15 METRES (50 FEET) TALL

LIFESPAN:
200 YEARS OR MORE

HABITAT:
SONORAN DESERT

THAT'S AMAZING!
DURING A RAINSTORM, A SAGUARO CACTUS CAN TAKE IN AND STORE MORE THAN A TONNE OF WATER. THAT'S ENOUGH TO FILL FOUR BATHS.

ARCTIC LUPIN

HEIGHT:
UP TO 50 CENTIMETRES (20 INCHES)

LIFESPAN:
A FEW YEARS

HABITAT:
ARCTIC MEADOWS AND HILLSIDES

THAT'S AMAZING!
THE SEEDS OF ARCTIC LUPINS LAST LONGER THAN THOSE OF OTHER PLANTS. SOME SEEDS WERE FOUND THAT WERE 10,000 YEARS OLD. WHEN THEY WERE PLANTED, THEY GREW.

POISON IVY

HEIGHT:
UP TO 1.5 METRES (5 FEET), BUT CAN GROW HIGHER UP ANOTHER PLANT

LIFESPAN:
SEVERAL YEARS

HABITAT:
WOODS, WASTE GROUND, ROADSIDES, AND HEDGEROWS

THAT'S AMAZING!
BURNING POISON IVY DOES NOT DESTROY ITS POISON. THE SMOKE FROM THE DRIED STEMS MAKES PEOPLE'S EYES SWELL SHUT.

HIGHBUSH BLUEBERRY

HEIGHT:
UP TO 4.5 METRES (15 FEET)

LIFESPAN:
MANY YEARS

HABITAT:
SWAMPS AND BOGGY WOODS

THAT'S AMAZING!
IN AUTUMN, SOME BLACK BEARS EAT ALMOST NOTHING BUT BLUEBERRIES. THEY CAN EAT ABOUT 10,000 BERRIES A DAY.

GIANT KELP

SIZE:
UP TO 50 METRES (164 FEET) LONG

LIFESPAN:
SEVERAL YEARS

HABITAT:
CLEAR SEA WATER

THAT'S AMAZING!
GIANT KELP GROWS VERY FAST. A FROND CAN GROW 60 CENTIMETRES (24 INCHES) IN A DAY.

Find out more

Books to read

Animals and Plants, Andrew Langley (Oxford University Press, 2002)

Plant Life Cycles, Anita Ganeri (Heinemann Library, 2006)

Plants and Planteaters (Secrets of the Rainforest), Michael Chinery (Crabtree Publishing Company, 2000)

Plants and the Environment, Jennifer Boothroyd (Lerner Publishing Group, 2007)

Plants that Eat Animals, Allan Fowler (Children's Press, 2001)

The Power of Plants, Claire Lewellyn (Oxford University Press, 2005)

The World's Largest Plants, Susan Blackaby (Picture Window Books, 2005)

Websites

www.kidsgeo.com/geography-for-kids/0153-biosphere.php
Learn more about weather, habitats, and how plants survive in them.

www.mbgnet.net/bioplants/adapt.html
Discover how plants adapt to different habitats, including deserts, grasslands, tropical rainforests, temperate forests, tundra, and water.

www.nanps.org/
A website that tells you about the native plants of North America.

www.plantcultures.org/
Find out about plants from all over the world at Kew Gardens' website.

Glossary

acid sour-tasting liquid

Arctic Ocean ocean surrounding the North Pole

bark hard outer layer of wood that covers a tree's trunk and branches

continent large area of land that includes many countries. There are seven continents in the world.

cultivated specially grown by farmers or scientists

desert place that gets very little rain and has very few plants

extinct no longer in existence

frond leaf of seaweed or fern

habitat place in the wild where particular types of plant grow and particular types of animal live

holdfast part of a kelp that attaches the seaweed to a rock

meadow grassy land, often near a river

nutrient part of food that is needed for health

plantation forest of trees or other plants that have been specially planted

pod container for seeds

poisonous something that is harmful if eaten or touched

pollen grains of yellow dust made by flowers

root part of a plant that takes in water and nutrients and anchors the plant in the soil

seed part of a plant that can grow into a new plant

species particular kind of living thing. Only members of the same species can produce new plants or animals of that species.

stem part of a plant on which leaves or flowers grow

swamp very wet, soft land

Index